# The
# Alchemy
## of
# Trust

*enjoy the book. Thank you for your help.*

## RESTORING TRUST
## In People and Organizations

*help.*

*Lynne Wainfan*

## Lynne Wainfan, Ph.D

Compass Alliance
Long Beach, California

Published by:

    Compass Alliance

    4358 Tulane Ave.

    Long Beach, CA 90808

ISBN 13: 978-0615660097

ISBN 10: 0615660096

**Cover and Text Design:** The Publishing Pro, LLC, Colorado Springs, California

**Author Photo:** Julie Wainfan

# Contents

Why Read This Book?     v

PART I — WHAT THE HECK HAPPENED?     1

    1. What Is Trust?     2

    2. Predictability     9

    3. Competence     12

    4. Values     15

    5. The Elemental Trust Model     20

    6. Case Study: Predictability     23

    7. Case Study: Competence     29

    8. Case Study: Values     42

PART II — TRUSTING WITHOUT BEING STUPID     57

    9. Assessing Trust     58

    10. Reality Check     67

    11. Failure to Recover     76

PART III — A VISION FOR THE FUTURE     85

    12. Organizational Accountability     86

    13. Go for the Gold     96

Bibliography     99

# Why Read This Book?

If you are reading this, then you know how to trust. You were born wide-eyed and hungry, and if you didn't trust, didn't open up your mouth, and make a decision to accept someone else's nourishment, you'd be dead by now.

Let's assume that you're not dead, but think about it: Life was golden then, wasn't it? You got everything you needed without thinking about it. But now you're not as trusting as you used to be, are you? You check your milk now to see if it's sour; when you're deciding important things, like who to vote for, you wrinkle your nose as you cast your ballot; you would never let a stranger give you a drink.

Thank goodness you weren't born this distrustful; you'd definitely be dead by now.

What the heck happened?

Life. When some product didn't turn as you predicted, or a person wasn't as competent as you thought, or you found out that someone might put something in your drink just to mess you up, it tore a little fiber out of your brain. To protect yourself, you began to adjust your belief in other people's trustworthiness downward.

You aren't alone. The world is in a crisis of trust. Gallup has been conducting polls on the subject for more than thirty-five years, and they are noticing that the U.S. as a nation has never been more distrustful of governments, financial institutions, and businesses.[1] More recently, other countries have noticed the same thing.[2]

What the heck happened?

Why are we less trusting than our parents were? Researchers have several theories: that the internet lets us see things before our government sees them; that the world is more complex; that jobs are harder than they used to be;

1.   Stevenson & Woolers, 2011

2.   Crête, Pelletier, & Couture, 2010; Cofta, 2009.

or that our more mobile society is putting us in contact with people whose values are very different from our own.[3]

I think people are just worn down. They're tired of getting their hopes up, only to have them bashed once again.

On the other hand, I think people are hoping to hope again. They want to trust and be trusted, and they're willing to read something that could help. At least I hope so. If you're reading this, then my hope was well placed and I thank you.

This book is written for anyone who has ever had their trust betrayed and wondered, "What the heck just happened?" It is also written for people who would like to trust more—without being stupid about it. Finally, it is written for those who would like to improve their little corner of the world, and maybe, just maybe, to influence others to be trustworthy as well.

The title of this book, *The Alchemy of Trust*, comes from a simple concept. Our trust may be at a low point, the basest of metals right now. But

---

3.  Bidner and Francois, 2011

here's the thing—we trusted once, we can trust again. It isn't rocket science.[4] I have worked with groups to help them understand what trust is, to repair their trust in each other, and to become more trustworthy. Distrust grinds you down like sand wears down an engine. Once you have a high-trust environment, life is golden. It's less wearing, more productive, and more fun.

If you and I improve trust in this world, even just a little … well, that's something.

Thank you for reading this far. I trust you'll enjoy the rest of the book.

---

4. Author is a former rocket scientist.

*PART I*

# What the Heck Happened?

---

*"Trust has been viewed as a somewhat mystical and intangible factor, probably defying careful definition"*
—K. Giffin

# ONE

# What Is Trust?

You have probably experienced a major breach of trust. You've likely been betrayed: stabbed in the back, dumped, fired, ripped off, or seriously pissed off. Hurts, doesn't it? If you're like me, you go through a process afterward. After the initial "ow," you try to figure out "what the heck just happened?" You try to make sense of the situation. If you're like me, you figure out what to do differently the next time.

This part of the book will help you understand what the heck just happened? The first chapter takes the nebulous, subjective concept of trust and makes it easier to understand. It defines trust as something that can be broken down into three elements that are easy to understand. The next few chapters take each of those elements and break *them* down, so you can pinpoint precisely what went wrong.

So what is trust? It is a subjective concept—one that exists in the trustor's mind, not by itself in the external world. Unlike a visible, tangible object, you can't point to trust sitting on the shelf and say, "There it is." Even though we were born doing it, we can't see it, touch it, or taste it.

Attempts to define trust seem to have failed, because academics in different fields think of trust in different contexts. Economists think of trust as two factors in a transaction between a trustor (the one doing the trusting) and a trustee (the one being trusted). Psychologists think of trust in terms of three factors that influence the trustor's decision to trust: the trustor's predisposition to trust, the circumstances, and the traits of the trustee.

This three-factor psychological framework seems attractive, but it doesn't quite ring true on the face of what we typically do. When we think about trust, we don't often think of our own predisposition to trust, and we don't often think about the circumstances. We just want to know if we can trust someone. When people talk about trust, they generally are thinking about someone else's trustworthiness.

So let's step back and see if we can create a framework for trust that is simple and understandable, one that we can actually use in our day-to-day lives.

If life is golden in a high-trust environment, let's think of trust as that bag of gold. The bag may be closed up and mysterious right now. Maybe your trust bag contains real gold, maybe the fool's gold of having been stupid about trust in the past. Who knows? What's in the bag? What is trust?

**FIGURE 1: What's in the bag?**

Let's open up that bag and see what other researchers have discovered about trust. The figure below shows a sampling of some of the words used in the different definitions of trust. (Notice how many there are—evidently, trust researchers don't trust each other's terms)

availability consistency dependability
predictability promise fulfillment
reliability responsiveness ability capability
competence confidence credibility expertise
good judgment altruism benevolence careful caring
concerned congruity cooperativeness discreetness fairness
favorable motives good intentions goodwill goodness honesty
integrity intentions keeping confidence loyalty morality
motive to not lie not manipulative not opportunistic
open-mindedness openness ownership of feelings
receptivity safeness shared values sincerity
values congruence

**FIGURE 2: Words used
in different definitions of trust**

These words have been put in three grouping; the technical word in systems theory for each of these columns is a clump. These clumps suggest three factors: predictability, competence, and values, as shown in the figure below.

What do these factors mean?

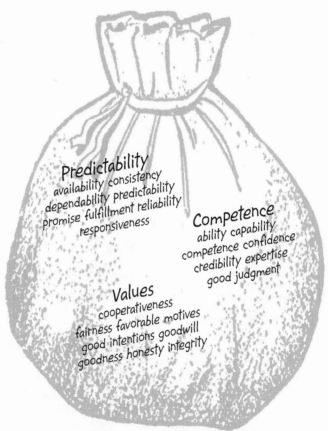

**FIGURE 3: Words used in different definitions of trust fall into three groups.**

- *Predictability* is how well future behavior can be anticipated.
- *Competence* is the ability to function successfully in a given domain.
- *Values* are principles and standards of behavior, judgment of what's important (what's of value).

So let's neaten up our trust model a bit. The figure below shows this top-level model of trust along with the definitions of the three factors of trust: predictability, competence, and values.

**FIGURE 4: The three factors of trust**

Okay, predictability is simple, and competence is somewhat understandable, but values are a bit complex. Just as we broke trust into three top-level factors, we can break each of these factors down further. We can take those sub-factors and break them down further and further until we arrive at something elemental.

Just like the gold in that ring of yours is an alloy of metals—gold, silver, copper, and possibly palladium—trust is a combination of the three factors: predictability, competence, and values. Those aren't quite defined down to their elemental levels yet, but we can keep going until the terms are so plain and clear as to be understandable and unambiguous.

The next chapters define these three factors of trust more completely, breaking each of them down further and further into their elemental levels. This will make them easier to understand, to talk about, and to assess. Using a quick and dirty assessment of the elements of the model, you will be able to pinpoint precisely what the heck went wrong.

# TWO

# *Predictability*

Predictability—how well future behavior can be anticipated—*is* trust to some people. My own observation is that men tend to equate trust with predictability more than women, but clearly it is an important component of trustworthiness. One of the earliest trust theorists defined trust "as an expectancy held by an individual or a group that the word, promise, verbal or written statement of another individual or group can be relied upon."[1]

An individual or organization can be predictable in two ways:

---

1.   Rottex, 1967.

- Meeting commitments—fulfilling promises, commitments, obligations in the future; or
- Behaving as expected when there are no prior commitments in place

Let's define these terms more precisely.

Meeting commitments: A commitment is a promise or obligation in the future. When we say, "She is committed to doing that," we mean that:

- there has been an explicit commitment; and
- the person is willing to meet that commitment.

If unforeseen circumstances pop up, she won't just stop. She will allocate resources; she will try to come up with ways to live up to her word.

Returning up one level in our model, the second sub-component of predictability is behaving as expected with no commitment in place. Although this expectation is often about something uncertain in the future, it could be an expectation of something else that's uncertain: behavior when the trustor isn't looking. "I trust that you're doing your homework," a mom might yell through a kid's closed door.

To summarize so far, the first component of trustworthiness is predictability. Its two elements are *meeting commitments* and *behaving as expected when there are no prior commitments in place*. The figure below shows this element of trustworthiness.

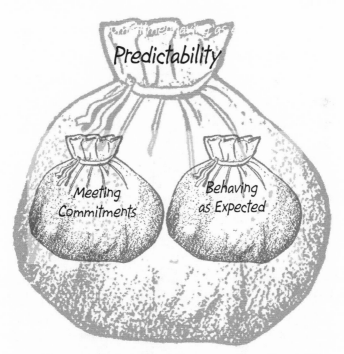

**FIGURE 5: The two components of predictability**

# THREE

# *Competence*

Competence is the ability to function successfully in some specific domain. This component of trust depends on the situation. You might trust the CEO to operate in the organization but not to operate on your appendix.

Just as we broke down predictability further, competence can be broken down into two sub-components:

- Ability
- Adaptability

Ability is the power or capacity to do something. In our example, it is Curt's ability as a chief executive officer to operate the nonprofit organization.

Ability itself can be broken down further into three sub-sub-components:

- *Aptitude*—innate, natural ability, type of intelligence, or special fitness for a task. It predicts how quickly something will be learned.
- *Training*—any form of education or instruction. It can be specific to a field (e.g., the department members all have medical degrees) or to a skill (e.g., listening skills).
- *Experience*—the accumulated knowledge that comes with time.

Returning up one level in our model, the second factor that makes up competence is adaptability. Adaptability is the ability to adjust to different conditions. For instance, a person or organization may need to adapt to changes in the demand for its products or services; in the availability of resources; or in its relationship with one or more stakeholders.

The figure below shows how competence, this second component of trustworthiness, breaks down into its sub-components.

**FIGURE 6: The two components of competence**

# FOUR

# *Values*

The third top-level component of trust is a bit more complex than either predictability or competence. Values are complex for a number of reasons, the first being that they're subjective or "squishy." Predictability and competence are easy to measure, using objective data. Second, you and I have a ton of values. Third, what you value changes, depending on your circumstance. If you're homeless in the rain, you value a piece of cardboard. If you're unpacking your new computer, you throw away the cardboard.

Okay, so values are complex. No big deal. We can desconstruct values just like we de-constucted competence. We'll look at what others have figured out and restructure those insights into something useful.

*The Oxford English Dictionary* says values are principles or standards of behavior; one's judgment of what is important in life.

Based on the trust and values research, the following sub-components of values are helpful in understanding trustworthiness:

- Benevolence
- Open-mindedness
- Carefulness
- Integrity

Let's walk through these factors one at a time and break them down further as needed.

<u>Benevolence</u> is the disposition to do good to others.

To be <u>open-minded</u>, according to the *Oxford Advanced Learners' Dictionary*, is to be "willing to listen to, think about or accept different ideas." This trait seems particularly important within small groups. I have encountered many people who are quite bright, often right, but not open-minded. They often see situations with great clarity and speak with conviction, but their lack of open-mindedness makes them distrusted by many of their group. They are seen as rigid and, at times, unreasonable.

Carefulness, related to conscientiousness, is giving attention to what you are doing so that you avoid hurting yourself or others, damaging something, or doing something wrong.

Integrity is the consistency between a person or organization's principles, words, and actions. In the novel, *To Kill a Mockingbird,* Atticus Finch explains to his daughter why he is defending Tom Robinson in court. His moral code demands consistency between his principles and the act of defending a black man—and in his words to his children: "If I didn't, I couldn't hold my head up in town. I couldn't even tell you or Jem not to do somethin' again."

Someone's lack of integrity is most visible when their words are inconsistent with their actions. Lack of integrity is obvious to any customer who hears, "Your call is important to us. Please hold."

So far we've taken some fuzzy components of trust and broken them down into clearer terms. Next, we'll put together the overall trust model

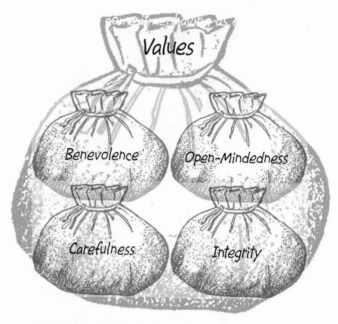

**FIGURE 7: The four components of values**

that includes all the elements of trust. We'll also
see how to use this model to figure out what the
heck happened.

Let's return to the first of these concepts, benevolence. It seems simple on the surface, but
is a difficult concept to understand and assess.
Let's break it down further.[1]

---

1.   Schwartz & Boehnke, 2004.

- *Honesty*—the trait of being truthful, sincere, and frank.
- *Loyalty*—a strong feeling of allegiance or support, of being faithful.
- *Helpfulness*—the desire to provide useful service
- *Responsibility*—being accountable for performing an action or role.

Okay, these elements are pretty basic, which means we can stop at this level. Figure 8 on page 21 shows how this third component of trustworthiness—values—breaks down into elemental sub-components.

FIVE

# *The Elemental Trust Model*

Trust has been broken down into its three top-level factors: predictability, competence, and values. Each of these factors has been broken down into one or more sub-factors. These in turn have been deconstucted further until we have a model of trust in its elemental form. Like elements in a periodic table, each term is basic, easy to understand and observe. The new, elemental model of trustworthiness is presented in the figure on the next page.

So what? What good does it do to have a model of trust down to its basic elements?

It helps you figure what the heck went wrong. You can look at the model and pinpoint the exact element that was problematic when your trust was breached. Once you know the

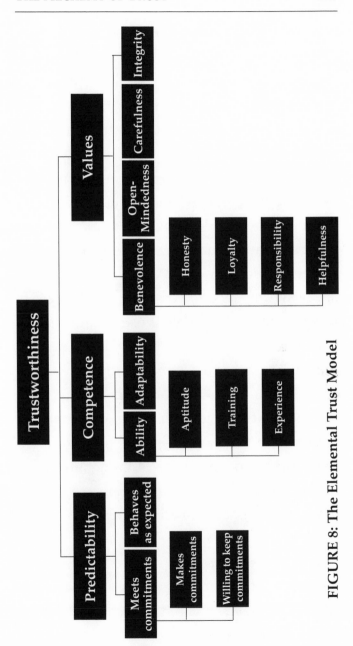

**FIGURE 8: The Elemental Trust Model**

specific area, it's easier to fix. You don't have to distrust completely, you can just get better at the problematic area. For instance, if the politician you voted for didn't meet commitments, you could check the next candidates' track record of meeting commitments. If your bank's website doesn't work with your cell phone, you could assess how adaptable they are. If the nonprofit organization you do volunteer work for has a scandal, you could evaluate the management's integrity.

Using this model, you can quickly identify the problematic elements. I use a simple color-code scheme. An element gets a black color rating if it is bad, a white for good, and a grey color rating if you don't know—it's a grey element.

The next chapters illustrate predictability, competence, and values—using real-world examples. In each of the cases, something went drastically wrong. See if you can use the model to figure out what the heck happened.

# SIX

# *Case Study: Predictability*

Thirty-three year old Jeremy Hill of Bonner's Ferry, Idaho, was in the shower on Mother's Day, 2011, when he heard his wife scream. Mrs. Hill had been looking out the bedroom window at four of their children playing basketball outside. "Get in the house!" she yelled at them. Jeremy Hill grabbed his daughter Jasmine's .270 rifle, loaded it, and followed his wife outside. There he saw three grizzly bears. One of the bears was climbing the wall of the family's pigpen. Hill fired a shot, hitting the grizzly, which fell off the fence and limped after the other two bears as they ran into the woods.

The family dog chased after the bear, which

turned and charged Hill as he stood near a large window under the deck of his house. Afraid that there was nothing except himself and a pane of glass to keep the wounded bear out of his house, Hill took aim and fired again.

Hill then went into the house to calm his wife and children and to call the Idaho Department of Fish and Game—except the grizzly wasn't dead. Knowing that a wounded bear posed a significant threat, Hill fired a final shot, killing the grizzly. The bear was forty yards from the basketball court where his children had been playing minutes before.[1]

Jeremy Hill thought he was protecting his family, but he has been charged with a federal crime. Killing a grizzly bear is punishable by up to one year in prison and a fine of $50,000. Grizzly bears were listed as threatened under the Endangered Species Act in 1975. In 2007, grizzlies were removed from the threatened list, but in 2009 a federal judge ordered protections restored because the government failed to ana-

1.   Spokesman Review, August 29, 2011, "Prosecutor Releases Details of N. Idaho Grizzly Killing,"

lyze the impact of climate changes on trout and high-elevation pines that provide food sources for grizzlies. That case is under appeal.[2]

The Jeremy Hill case illustrates the difficulty of predicting the effects of policy. As U.S. Representative Raul Labrador, who represents Hill's district said, "Clearly, we have a problem with the Endangered Species Act when situations like this happen."

The federal government's act of charging Hill with a crime came after other officials went on the record in support. State officials took no action against Hill. "It seems unjust to me that someone would be charged when they were protecting their family," said Idaho State Senator Shawn Keough. "I'm at a loss to understand why the U.S. government is pursuing this in the manner they are." Supporters have contributed $20,000 to Hill's defense, and so many came to his hearing that it had to be moved to a larger courtroom. Idaho senator Jim Risch, a former prosecutor said, "What Mr. Hill did was not a criminal act in the court of common sense.

2. Zuckerman, 2011

My hope is that common sense prevails in this case."[3] The commissioners in Idaho's Boundary County issued a statement supporting Hill, saying that he, "not only had the right, but the obligation to protect his children and his family."[4]

Many feel that the government's prosecution of Hill defies explanation. Let's see if we can use the elemental trust model to figure out what the heck went wrong.

Recall that the three factors of trust are predictability, competence, and values. Let's start by assessing predictability: Was the government's prosecution of Hill predictable? Let's drill a little deeper and see if we can pinpoint the problem. In our elemental trust model, predictability has two subfactors: meeting commitments, and behaving as expected with no commitment in place.

It may have been predictable that a man would shoot a bear that had threatened his children, but it certainly wasn't predictable that the government would prosecute him for it. In fact,

3.   Barker, 2011

4.   Gould, 2011

the government's lack of predictability is precisely what the federal, state, and local officials were complaining about. Clearly, the government acted in an unpredictable way—they get a black rating for predictability.

The other factors, competence and values can be left grey for now, since they haven't been assessed. As an aside, can we predict what might

**FIGURE 9: Regarding Jeremy Hill, government earns a black rating for predictability.**

happen if the government keeps acting unpredictably? There is some precedent: The founding fathers revolted when a king took away their liberties and did not redress their grievances. They designed a government based on a written constitution, and established checks and balances to prevent individuals from violating others' liberties. As the founding fathers so capably demonstrated, when governments become sufficiently untrustworthy, new governments take their places.

# SEVEN

# Case Study: Competence

Joseph Berardino's large brown eyes watched Louisiana Congressman Richard Baker lean towards the microphone. The congressman introduced him to a room that was a flurry of motion, with cameramen and members of the congressional committee hurrying back from their break in order to hear his testimony. Berardino cleared his throat and glanced at the paper in front of him. His company's lawyers had reviewed his written statement, he had read the document several times, and he knew what to say. As he started to talk, he found that his voice was not quite there. Clearing his throat, Berardino started to talk once more. "Good afternoon," he said hoarsely. "Thank you for inviting me to appear before you today. I'm here because faith in our firm and the integrity of the capital market system has been shaken."

Berardino, 51, looked more like Boy Scout troop master than CEO of global accounting firm Andersen Worldwide. His hair was longer than the stereotypical accountant, and today he wore an American flag on his lapel. He glanced up at the dark-suited elected officials before him and then continued to read from his prepared statement. "Andersen will not hide from its responsibilities."

Almost thirty years before, Berardino had sat in corporate training as had every other Andersen new hire for almost sixty years before him. They had all heard the same story, the legendary tale that had set the tone for the auditing industry.

The story he heard went like this: In 1914, a railroad executive had burst into Arthur Andersen's tiny reception area, insisting that Andersen approve his corporate financial ledger. Andersen countered that there was not enough money in the city of Chicago to make him approve bad bookkeeping. The small accounting firm lost a big client, but the railroad went bankrupt a few months later. Andersen, vindicated, had established a reputation for integrity. Since then, Andersen Worldwide had enjoyed eighty-eight years of prosperity, primarily for taking tough stands on accounting issues. Anderson Worldwide's integrity would enrage clients while making them the auditing firm that financial investors could trust.

Auditors are called "the guardians of the public trust." They are knowledgeable about the rules of finance and how to enforce them. If an auditing firm signs a company's financial statement, it assures the public that the company is following the rules and adhering to financial standards of conduct. An auditor's signature helps the public decide whether to trust a company enough to invest.

Now Joseph Berardino was being called upon to explain to congressional leaders and the world what the heck had gone wrong. His firm had been paid $52 million the previous year to audit Enron's finances.[1] Flipping the page, Berardino got to the heart of his statement. "Our team has made an error in judgment." The firm

---

1.   Manor and Yates, 2002.

responsible for judging companies' accounting practices had failed to do its job.

Enron's illegal accounting activities, undetected by Berardino's auditing firm, caused the largest bankruptcy to date—$65 billion.[2] Four months later, Andersen would become the first auditing firm in history to be criminally convicted. Although the felony conviction would later be overturned, the damage to Andersen Worldwide was already fatal. Since the U.S. Securities and Exchange Commission does not allow convicted felons to audit public companies, the firm surrendered its CPA licenses and sold off most of its operations to competitors. Andersen went from 85,000 employees worldwide to 200, most of those dealing with lawsuits and the dissolution of the firm.

What the heck happened?

How did a financial institution go from being the most respected guardian of the public trust to having its CEO testifying before congress?

Enron, the company that the Andersen firm audited, committed illegal accounting acts;

---

2.　　Jenkins, 2003 .

that is not disputed. The question is why the nonstandard practices were not caught by the Andersen's auditing team. The answer, surprisingly, is that they were.

At Andersen, there are three types of specialties: partners assigned to each client; professional standards group; and practice directors.[3] The partners assigned to each client are the ones who sign the audit statements for Andersen, certifying that they meet accounting standards. The professional standards group consists of the technical experts who understand the accounting standards and rules—and how they are enforced. They keep current on the regulatory and legal changes as well as any methodological changes that may occur in accounting. The third specialty group at Anderson consisted of the practice directors. They look across Andersen's portfolio clients, evaluating the risk the clients provide, and whether Andersen has the right people assigned to each client.

A member of the professional standards group wrote what has been called the smoking

---

3.   PBS, 2002

gun email. On February 1, 2000, Carl Bass sent his boss a list of issues that he had with "a complicated series of Enron derivatives." Among them, "Derivatives cannot hedge derivatives for accounting purposes."[4] Bass reported that he had discussed these issues with the partner assigned to the client, David Duncan.

A few months after his congressional testimony, Berardino explained Andersen's management process for handling such cases:[5]

> What is supposed to happen is that there is to be an agreement, and if any partner is uncomfortable with advice we're giving a client, I expect them to keep going up the chain until they get comfortable … In a partnership, we operate through consensus. So if everyone agrees with the answer, life is easy. If there are disagreements, those disagreements are supposed to bubble up in the organization either on a case-by-case basis—we're discussing this accounting is-

---

4.   CNN, 2002

5.   PBS, 2002

sue with that accounting issue—or when we decide whether or not we're going to retain a client. All this is intended to give our line partner, who serves the client in the field, the best answers as quickly as possible in some very highly complex situations … if there's a disagreement, it would go up through our hierarchy in the firm. We have a leadership in each office. We have a leadership in the country. The two kinds of disagreements would be either in a specific accounting issue or should we keep this client. At the end of the day, frankly, we are able to reach consensus. That's how we've tried to do it.

Unfortunately, this is not what happened. Instead of the disagreement going up the chain until agreement was reached, Carl Bass was removed from the project by the Andersen partner assigned to the client. When Berardino was asked about this, he replied:

Well, it's very unusual that we would remove somebody. I was not consulted on that decision, I don't know all the factors that went into it. But at times, frankly, we have people who don't perform, and at times we have people who do perform, and clients object to both. You've got to make a judgment call.

At the end of the day, and they'd alter the relationship to some extent, although it's a skeptical relationship, you do rely on trust in each other. The client wants to feel that you're understanding their business problem, that you're understanding what they're trying to accomplish with their accounting for business transactions. If you have people that either don't have the bedside manner, don't have the capability, don't have the expertise to get in a client's shoes to understand it, clients react negatively. OK? Then we've got to make a judgment call as to whether they're objecting to that service for the right reason or the wrong reasons. It's very rare that we remove somebody. Obviously, this was one of those rare situations.

What the heck went wrong here?

Let's apply our elemental model of trust to see if we can pinpoint the problem precisely.

Recall the top-level factors of trust: Predictability, Competence, and Values. Was this a problem of predictability? Perhaps. But just as in the bear-shooting case, there was a bureaucratic system in place to weed out corruption. Were accounting problems predicted? Yes. There is no smoking gun here.

The second factor in the trust model is competence. Recall that competence can be broken down into ability and adaptability. But whose competence shall we assess? Let's assess Anderson as an organization.

What is an organization? It is a collection of individuals and an organizational structure—policies and procedures—to support the individuals' actions.

Andersen clearly employed individuals who were capable—Carl Bass caught several of Enron's accounting problems, after all. Andersen also had the organizational structure for technical ability in their professional standards group. So they had at least one highly compe-

tent individual, along with an organizational
structure to support that individual, but they
still failed to competently audit Enron. This
is curious and ambiguous, so let's say that for
the moment, we can't assess Anderson's ability.
It's okay to leave a factor grey and move on to
easier ones.

Looking to the right of ability in the elemental trust model (see Figure 8), the next
subfactor to assess is adaptability. We have
reason to believe that Andersen scored high
here. Their technical standards group was
well known for keeping current on the latest
accounting standards and practices and regulatory changes. Some of their partners served
on standards boards, leading those changes.
Andersen technical experts were well respected in the field and could be expected to be on
top of any technical changes. There were some
questions of conflict of interest among the so-
called "big five" consulting firms: the so-called
fox watching the chicken house system where
auditors are paid by the clients they oversee.
But all auditing firms face the same conflict,
and the system had worked pretty well for

eighty-eight years. As Berardino described above, Andersen had a process in place to resolve another conflict—the natural tensions that arise between the technical experts and the client managers. Thus, their adaptability rates a white.

So we return to the factor we couldn't assess—ability—to see if there's a smoking gun there. In Chapter 3, we saw that ability can be characterized as aptitude, training, and experience. Clearly Carl Bass had the technical aptitude, training, and experience to detect and notify his superiors about Enron's accounting problems. This technical ability is necessary but not sufficient in an organization; it must be accompanied by management ability. According to congressional testimony, Andersen's client partner, David Duncan, went to higher-level partners requesting that Bass be removed from the project. His request was approved and Bass was reassigned.

This single management decision, recommended by an individual but ratified by upper management, was the root cause of the failure. Anderson clearly failed to do the job they were hired to do: to audit Enron. The Arthur Andersen partners were not competent to make the same call that Arthur Andersen himself had made almost nine decades earlier with the railroad company.

So Anderson's failure was in ability. This element of competence gets a black rating, and therefore competence gets a bad, or black, rating as shown below.

**FIGURE 10: Arthur Andersen rated highly for its adaptability but earned a black rating for ability.**

An interviewer recently asked Berardino whether he loses sleep about ignoring Carl Bass' warnings. His response: "I sleep like a baby. I wake up every two hours and cry."

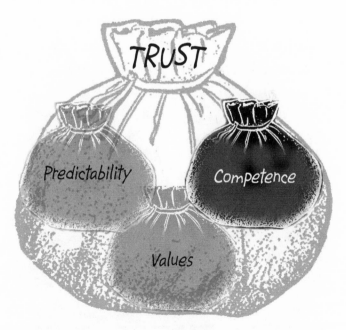

**FIGURE 11: Arthur Andersen scored badly in competence because of its management ability.**

EIGHT

# Case Study: Values

Oprah Winfrey put the phone down in her Chicago apartment, shaken to the core. She would later describe this as the most devastating episode of her life. [1]

Oprah had already overcome many difficulties in her fifty-three years. She had been born in rural Mississippi to a single teenage mother. After her birth, her mother moved north, leaving Oprah with her grandmother. Oprah was so poor, she wore potato sacks, a source of teasing by the local children. When she was six, she

1. CBC News, November 6, 2007. http://www.blinkx. com/watch-video/oprah-winfrey-press-conference/ 9f5Kqqck8lkZGMJdC73e8w

moved to Milwaukee to live with her mother who worked long hours as a maid. Two years later, she was moved to Tennessee, to live with the man believed to be her father. Oprah reports being molested by her cousin, uncle, and a family friend, beginning at age nine. At age thirteen, Oprah ran away from home, and became pregnant at fourteen. Her son died shortly after birth.

Her life started to turn with her focus on education. She returned to Tennessee, became an honors student, and worked in a grocery store. She won a full scholarship to Tennessee State University, majoring in communication while broadcasting the news at a local radio station.

Oprah Winfrey is credited with revolutionizing the talk show format. Instead of Donahuetype "report-talk," walking among audience members with a microphone, she uses "rapport-talk"—sitting alongside her guests, sympathizing with them, often crying with them.[2]

Now, as she finished her phone call with the chief executive of the Oprah Winfrey Leadership

2.    Time magazine, 1998

Academy for Girls in South Africa, Oprah cried.[3] The executive had just told her that a student had run away from the boarding school Oprah had founded. Fifteen girls had come forward with accusations that a dorm matron had mistreated the girls. One of the girls said she'd been sexually assaulted.

Oprah had created the school to give back to the community what she'd been given by her grandmother—a desire for an education.[4] Had her school instead given back something else—sexual assault?

The idea for the school started seven long years before, in 2000. While visiting Nelson Mandela, the first democratically elected president of impoverished South Africa, Oprah had been inspired. "I want to create a school for smart girls who will lead this country into glory," she told him. Two years later, a site for the boarding school was selected and groundbreaking took place in tiny Henley on Klip near Johannesburg. Attending the groundbreaking

---

3.   *The Guardian,* November 5, 2007

4.   Press Conference

ceremony were Nelson Mandela, Spike Lee, and Tina Turner. Oprah told the crowd, "When you change a girl's life, it's not just that life. You start to affect a family, a community, a nation. I'm telling you, women are going to change the face of Africa."

The plans for the school grew as Oprah became involved with the details. Oprah rejected drawings for facilities that she thought were substandard. "I am creating everything in this school that I would have wanted for myself—so the girls will have the absolute best that my imagination can offer." The 52-acre campus grew to include twenty-eight buildings, including dormitories, a dining hall, libraries, two theaters, and a wellness center. Oprah's investment grew from $10 million to $100 million She wanted to provide the girls with a setting that inspired them to dream beyond what their life had shown them so far. "[I]f you are surrounded by beautiful things and wonderful teachers who inspire you, that beauty brings out the beauty in you."[5]

---

5.   Euroweb, January 3, 2007

Oprah's involvement with the school grew as the school came closer to admitting students. "I went to some of their homes," she reported in a 2007 interview, "I've met with their teachers, I've met with their parents, I've met with them. I know them all by name. I know their stories because their story is my story. And what I do know for sure is that this school is going to change the trajectory of their lives."[6]

Some observed that Oprah came to see these girls as the daughters that she never had. "When I first started making a lot of money, I really became frustrated with the fact that all I did was write cheque after cheque to this or that charity without really feeling like it was a part of me," Oprah told *Newsweek* magazine. "At a certain point, you want to feel that connection." She visited the school often, saying it was, "the most vital aspect of my life." By the time she announced the end of her talk show, she reportedly was building a home for herself on the campus to spend time with the girls and to be involved in their education: "I love these

6.   NPR, January 2007

7.   Washington Post, January 2007

girls with every part of my being."[7]

Twenty-two months before Oprah received the devastating phone call, she'd made a promise she could not keep: "I said to the mothers, the family members, the aunts, the grannies—because most of these girls have lost their families, their parents—I said to them, 'Your daughters are now my daughters and I promise you I'm going to take care of your daughters. I promise you.' "[8]

How could Oprah, considered by many to be the most powerful woman in the world,[9] a person who had personally overseen every detail of this worthy cause, find herself in this situation?

What the heck went wrong?

We can apply the elemental trust model to assess where the problem may have originated. Recall that there are three top-level components of trust: predictability, competence, and values. I like to remember them with an acronym, PCV.

---

8.   ABC News, January 3, 2006

9.   The Telegraph, October 31, 2007

Was this a failure of predictability? Maybe so: Oprah clearly didn't predict this. In a sense, it was a failure of predictability because it was unpredictable. But then again, breached trust *is* unpredictable, otherwise it isn't such a breach, it's more like an economic exchange where expected outcomes could be assessed beforehand. Unlike the bear shooting case a few chapters ago, where the bureaucracy of the federal government did not behave in a way that was predictable, there was no vast system of checks and balances at the school to weed out corruption. Predictability is hard to assess here, so let's assess the lower-level sub-factors within predictability:

- Meeting commitments: fulfilling promises, commitments, obligations in the future; or
- Behaving as expected when there are no prior commitments in place

Looking at these terms, it's still hard to say. Clearly there was an implicit commitment in place, to treat the girls with respect. We do have some facts though: Someone had put procedures in place for the students to redress their grievances. We know that because girls did indeed come forward. Therefore, someone had predicted that there might be misconduct and had put the procedures in place to bring it to light. From this, we can deduce that this was not a failure to predict, therefore predictability gets a white rating.

Moving on to the second factor in PCV, we

**FIGURE 12: The Leadership Academy did well in the predictability component.**

assess competence. But whose competence? Oprah herself believed that there had been a failure in the "school's systems."[10] What does that mean? Systems theory suggests that there are a variety of clumps here: the dorm matron, her boss, the headmistress, the students, and others.

Was the dorm matron who allegedly abused the girls competent? Court records document that Winfrey admitted she had planned to hire nurses to be dorm matrons for the school. Instead, the headmistress hired eight women from a company called Party Design. Oprah's lawyers said, "These young women were later found to be totally unqualified to handle the position, something the headmistress had been warned about."

Let's imagine that the dorm matron was not competent to handle the position. Even so, she could have been competent to not abuse the girls. Was she? We drill down in our model and look at the factors underneath competence: ability and adaptability. Was the dorm matron able

---

10.. *Guardian*, UK.

to not abuse the girls? Likely so. Was this an adaptability problem? Hard to say.

Let's look at some facts. The dorm matron was charged with fourteen counts of abuse against six students. She had a history of problems with the school, and was alleged to attack a colleague and injuring three people while driving a golf cart after a champagne party. She also retaliated against girls who complained of mistreatment.

This suggests that there was a failure to correct a problem employee's behavior. The headmistress would have been responsible to do this, and she was the one who hired dorm matrons from a company called Party Design. Therefore, her competence could definitely be called into question. Was this whole episode due to the incompetence of the headmistress? Hard to say. Clearly, the dorm matron contributed more to the problem than the headmistress. Let's leave the headmistress' competence grey for the moment and continue with our trust assessment of the other parts of the system, the students.

The girls demonstrated their competence in

speaking out about the mistreatment. In fact, the dorm matron had been accused of retaliating against a student for speaking out, but others came forward and nine girls testified against her. The students get a white rating for competence.

Thus, the dorm matron's competence was left grey, as was the headmistress' competence, and the students' competence got a white rating.

The third factor in the elemental model of trust is values. Recall that there are some subfactors:

**FIGURE 13: The Leadership Academy's overall competence was mixed and was left grey.**

- Benevolence
- Open-mindedness
- Carefulness
- Integrity

Let's walk through these factors one at a time and break them down further as needed.

The dorm matron's benevolence—her disposition to do good to others—had been called into question many times. She was alleged to have attacked a colleague, to injure people with a golf cart, and to abuse six students. Clearly, her benevolence deserves a black rating.

What about open-mindedness? Again, the facts are sketchy—retaliating against girls who came forward is not very benevolent, but we don't have enough data to give a rating other than grey here.

Carefulness deserves a black rating because the headmistress did not take reasonable care to correct the dorm matrons' behavior.

Integrity is a little more difficult to assess— was there deceit? Since we have little information about this factor, it gets a grey rating.

The figure below shows the assessment of

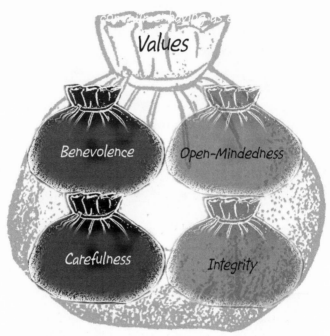

**FIGURE 14: The Leadership Academy earned black marks for 2 of the values components.**

the values of the organization, which are given a black rating because of the extreme lack of benevolence and carefulness demonstrated.

Rolling the ratings upward in our trust model, we see that the values component is the source of the problem, due to the benevolence issue. We have found our smoking gun.

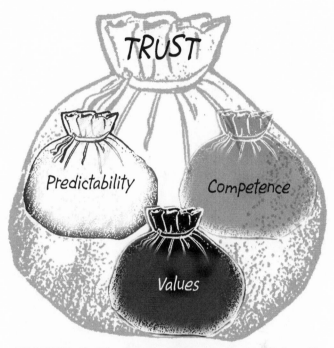

**FIGURE 15: The Leadership Academy did well with the predictability factor but failed in the values area.**

*PART II*
# Trusting Without Being Stupid

---

*"Trust in me."*
—Ka, the snake from *Jungle Book*

# NINE

## *Assessing Trust*

### THE TYPICAL PROCESS

Think back to an incident when your trust was breached in a way that you'll never forget. Perhaps it was that first school yard bully. Maybe it was your first true love who dumped you. Was it an organization you worked for? One you invested in? Think back to the one that sticks out as the worst, the one that affects you still today.

Got one? Okay, now think about what the universe was trying to teach you with that one. Was it that you should never trust a fifth grader? That men are pigs (or women bitches)? That corporations are evil? That the stock market is unpredictable?

If you're like most people, you learn lessons from breached trust. You learn to be more careful the next time. You learn to not trust at all. Or you learn to _____ (fill in the blanks). The problem is, the more often your trust is betrayed, the more fill-in-the-blanks there are. If you live long enough, you will find that all men, all women, all organizations, all institutions, and all schemes are not to be trusted.

So that's what the heck happened. The reason the world is in a crisis of trust is that we've lived long enough.

Isn't that galling? Age is supposed to bring wisdom, grandchildren, and retirement. You are wise to the point of not trusting anyone, your grandchildren are ungrateful louts, and you can't retire because you can't predict your cost of living.

## A BETTER PROCESS

Now that we know more about trust, we can more accurately figure out what the heck happened in that noteworthy breach you have in mind. Think back. Was it a problem with predictability? Competence? Values? Well, which one was it?

## STEP 1: Assess What the Heck Happened

Let's work through some examples to illustrate a better process of figuring out what happened. Let's start with the last guy you voted for president. Was he elected? Did he do what you thought he would? If he lost, did you think that he would lose? This would be a problem with predictability.

Next, consider a place where you used to like to work. The work was cool, the people nice, and the pay was better than you'd hoped for. Something went wrong, perhaps in a performance appraisal. Maybe you missed a promotion, or maybe coworkers let you down. Was the management competent? Did they anticipate problems and have the policies, practices, and procedures in place to deal with these very predictable problems? If not, then this was a failure of competence.

Finally, let's imagine that your first love broke your heart. What went wrong there, anyways? Perhaps your love wasn't as benevolent as you had imagined—looking out too often for his or her interests instead of yours. Perhaps this person lied, cheated on you, or showed some other lack of integrity. If so, then the breach of trust was that their values didn't line up with yours.

## STEP 2: Own Your Piece of the Problem

It is quite common for people to blame the person who breached their trust rather than themselves. And many times this is appropriate. The schoolyard bully may have been bullied himself, perhaps at home, but that's no excuse to continue the cycle of violence.

On the other hand, it is helpful to "own" your piece of any bad interaction. Owning your piece of problem means reaching down into yourself and identifying what part, if any, you played.

Let's illustrate this with our examples from before.

Your presidential candidate was, after all, your guy. You voted for him. You had plenty of chances to study him or her during the campaign; tons of information were available to you to study the candidates, their backgrounds, their positions on the issues, their past predictability. Then too, you probably have heard that candidates don't always keep their promises. Well, shame on you then. If this is you thinking back on your presidential candidate's unpredictability, then you *did* have some information, didn't you?

Now consider the example of the workplace situation gone bad. Did the person who breached your trust have all the information to manage the situation? Did you bring it to someone's attention early enough for something to be done? Could you have just kept your head down and done your job? The situation may have blown over.[1] These are a few of the things you could own about the bad interaction. There are likely many more.

Finally, let's talk about that first love who broke your heart. Okay, you might not be ready to own any of that, especially if your heart is still out of whack, but you may find that perhaps you didn't account for the lover's "soft spots," areas where

---

1.   I have a theory that 99 percent of the things we worry about don't need us worrying about them. The problem may be solved by someone else, it may go away, or there might not be anything you can do about it anyways. Time and feedback loops are excellent healers.

they weren't as good as you'd like. Nobody's perfect, and maybe you expected too much. People's values change with time—perhaps you and your lover valued the same things at the beginning of your relationship but your values diverged with time. People evolve, you know.

Okay, now that we have the hypothetical examples, go ahead and try it—own your piece of the terrible breached trust that you thought of a few pages ago.

Think back as specifically as possible about a situation where a person or organization who breached your trust. Who was the person who did you wrong? What were your feelings for them? How much did you trust them--with your car? your money? your home? your dog? your secrets? What were the relevant circumstances: were you poor? lonely? Did you have reason to trust/distrust this person or organization? Take a moment and list all the things about the other party—and about the trust breach situation.

Now think about the action that this person or organization took that betrayed your trust. Be as specific as possible. For example, "She stole my cockatoo when I was at work and lied to me when she told me a burglar did it." Or "He promised me a raise in two months, and after a year I still didn't have it." Perhaps it was more like, "The technician swore he'd be done by noon so I could pick up my daughter and he wasn't done until three o'clock," or "The company mailed me something that smelled so bad I had to put it in the other room." It would be helpful to write down how exactly your trust was betrayed.

Now here's the hard part: owning your piece of the breach. The thinking you did above was all about facts: what you trusted someone with; and how they betrayed your trust. This next part is about conjecture. What part of the breach did you contribute to? Here are some questions that might help you identify your part of the problem:

- Was the arrangement "too good to be true?"
- Was there information out there that could have told me this might happen?
- Could I have seen this coming? How?
- Did I have any warning this might happen?

- Had something like this happened to me before?
- Did the person or organization give me an inkling that this might happen?
- Could I have done something to check my assumptions?
- If I had been perfect, would this still have happened to me?
- Would the other person/organization admit they were wrong?
- Would they say I contributed to the problem? How?

From these questions, as well as any other thoughts you might have on the subject, you can identify your part of the trust breach you experienced.

**STEP 3: Do something**

As mentioned earlier, it is easy for people to over-generalize when they get hurt. They are so cautious about not getting hurt again that they make sweeping generalizations—politicians are crooked, businesses are out to get the little guy, women are bitches, men are idiots. Now that you've had a chance to drill a bit deeper, you might find that you can come up with a more nuanced resolution to your terrible breach.

A good place to start is with the piece that you own. Perhaps instead of distrusting all politicians, you can do a bit more research the next time. Perhaps by just watching a workplace situation go bad, you can do something about it (or not do something, if you contributed to the problem). The next time you choose a lover, look past your initial impression to decide if their values line up with yours.

TEN

*Reality Check*

The earlier sections of this chapter provide a process to trust without being stupid about it, but in the real world sometimes a process isn't enough. I've shown you the way, but you must have the will. From my experience, this takes time, and rushing it along doesn't always result in a fair assessment. We humans are very good at getting out of "dissonance," the gap between our beliefs and our perceptions.

One helpful approach is to get a second opinion about who to trust. After all, you consult another physician before surgery, right? How about getting a reality check from someone you trust before writing off the government/businesses/people?

The problem with reality checks is that no one really knows what reality is. Physicist Stephen Hawking says that we all create our own reality. This is a bit scary, because your reality might be different from mine. Yikes!

I agree with Hawking, but I have a model of reality that makes me feel better. This model starts with everything that is within you—your mind, your physical self, and your heart, even the cavity that hasn't gone away because you don't trust dentists. Everything you can conceive that is inside of you.

Now imagine everything that is outside of you—that politician who disappointed you, your coworkers, that old love—but things other than people as well: nature, newspapers, radio waves, sunlight, and on and on. This is a bit tougher to wrap your mind around because everything outside you is so vast—infinitely so, in fact.

Okay, so we've got everything inside you and everything outside you. Clear so far? Let's complicate it just a bit by describing how those two things interact. The figure on the next page shows a simplified model of reality.

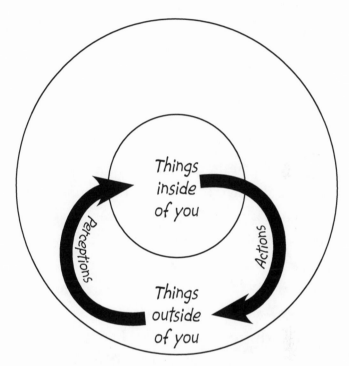

**FIGURE 15: A Simplified Model of Reality**

The things going from yourself are your actions. These are the things you do to mess with things outside of yourself—you vote, you commute, you ask someone out on a date. Actions are verbs. To do, to be, to read, or not to read, that is the question.

Your perceptions, how you take in things outside of you, are the key to understanding your reality and that of others.

## PERCEPTIONS VARY

Your perceptions are a little more difficult to break down analytically. My generation was taught that there are five senses: sight, smell, taste, sound, and touch. To paraphrase the nobel laureate John Nash, this model is incomplete, gentlemen, incomplete. For instance, we now know that smell and taste are related—ever eaten something when you had a cold? Try this—plug your nose and taste something. Not so great tasting, is it?

Similarly, researchers now know that sight is affected by your cognitive biases. Elizabeth Loftus, a researcher at University of California Irvine, did some amazing studies to show that seeing is not necessarily believing. In one experiment, subjects were separated into two groups and shown a video of a car accident. The first group was asked, "About how fast were the cars going when they smashed into each other?" The second group was asked, "About how fast were the cars going when they hit each other?"

Did you catch it? The only difference between the two sentences was the word *smashed* vs. the word *hit*.

Later they came back and were asked, "Did you see any broken glass?"

Here are the results. The first group, the ones who were asked about *smashing* cars were twice as likely to see broken glass as the ones who had been asked about *hitting* cars. That single word difference, *smash* vs. *hit*, caused twice as many people to say that there was broken glass in the accident. One word changed the second group's perception.

But here's the weird thing: There was *no* broken glass—32 percent of the *smashed* group and 14 percent of the *hit* group said they saw glass that was not there. These are eye witnesses, mind you, and both groups saw broken glass because they believed there was.

Your perception is your reality, and it isn't necessarily the same as objective reality. As you can see from the above experiment, people's reality varies.

So what is reality? Many people say that they trust their senses. Makes sense, doesn't it (literally)? These are your connection points with the world outside you, after all. Didn't you learn that there are five senses?

Nowadays, at least in California, they are teaching the kids in school that there are more than five senses. That old "sixth sense" that we heard about in hushed tones is now called intuition. But wait, there's more: a sense of hunger, a sense of thirst, a sense of how your body moves, this list is ever-growing. When they get to studying a sense of humor in third grade, I want to be a teacher's aide for the spitballs alone.

So you can see that the concept of perception is more complex than just your senses. In the broken-glass experiment, your perception of what you see is affected by what you hear. How weird is that? There are more than five senses and in fact there is no agreed-upon model for how many senses we have.

Great. If your perception of things outside yourself is fuzzy, what does that say about your reality? A few things. First, that it's fuzzy also. If you were in the one group that saw the accident video, you'd be convinced there was broken glass. Your roommate in the other group would be just as convinced that there was no broken glass at all.

The second thing you can say about perceptions is that people differ. Just because you perceive something to be real, it doesn't mean that the guy sitting next to you will perceive the same thing. *Quelle bummaire!* Your reality is different from that of the guy sitting next to you.

And in fact what you attend to—what you choose to look at and think about—is different from everyone else's also. You may see a shooting star and be frustrated that your shy husband was looking at his shoes. (If he's particularly outgoing, he might be looking at *your* shoes.) In that moment, you would have a different reality from him—your reality would include a shooting star, his would be focused on an untied shoelace.

So you can imagine that when something like a breached trust incident occurs, the person doing the breaching might have a different perception of the event than the one whose trust was breached. That first love of yours, the one who wasn't very considerate? She probably thought you weren't very adventurous. That manager who didn't deal with the problem employee? She was probably worried about the budget cuts. The presidential candidate? Well, who knows what they think about—other than sex?

## THE FUNDAMENTAL ATTRIBUTION ERROR

There is an intriguing concept in psychology called the fundamental attribution error. We all make this error, and the strange thing is that we can't all be right. The fundamental attribution error is illustrated by the following example. You're meeting someone for lunch. If you happen to be late, it's due to circumstances beyond your control—things outside yourself like traffic. If *he's* late, it's due to something innate—something inside *him*—like *his* disregard for your time. As far as *your* failures, nothing is *your* fault—it's all outside of you. If your opposite number thinks the same way, which people generally do, then you can't both be right.

So the key point here is that just because your trust was breached, and you think you know why, the breachor's experience might have been different. You probably think you were the victim, and he was the jerk. Now that you know how to own your piece of that difficulty, that's good. What is important is to consider the big picture, not just the things inside yourself, but the things outside yourself as well. Only then can you hope to be in touch with reality.

And in reality, people generally don't go about *trying* to breach trust—it happens and they probably had some sort of rationale for doing it. People are very rational creatures. In fact, they can rationalize anything.

## MAKING SENSE OF THE BREACH

The final step is to make better sense of the breach. Instead of distrusting all women/corporations/politicians, maybe you can pinpoint the elemental problem—*she* wasn't predictable, *they* weren't competent, *he* wasn't benevolent. From there, you can get better at perceiving what *you* missed before. You don't have to throw the baby out with the bath water. You can identify the elements of trust—predictability, competence, or values—that were problematic and work on trusting better the next time.

The next chapter describes some people who couldn't recover. Now that you've read this far, you are probably smarter than they were. I trust that you won't let this happen to you.

# ELEVEN

# *Failure to Recover*

## PATHOLOGY OF A TRUST FATALITY

Recall the premise at the beginning of this book, that you start out life as a trusting being. You *have* to trust in order to open your mouth and take nourishment from others. Something happens—life, probably—that turns you into someone not as trusting. And you're not alone: We are in a global crisis of trust, worse than any time in the past thirty-five years at least, perhaps more.

What is the diagnosis for our condition?

It's hard to answer this question for you as an individual because, as we saw in the last few chap-

ters, you have some work to do if you want to recover from breached trust. But we can certainly look
at the data that are out there about organizations.

You are all familiar with at least one organization that went out of business, right? The
exemplar used in business schools is the hypothetical buggy-whip factory. Its cause of death
is quite clear—a new and unforeseen event, the
birth of the automobile, just whacked the poor
little buggy-whip factory out of existence.

But wait, couldn't they have foreseen something, or at least foreheard it? The automobile age
was pretty hard to miss, with cars rattling down
the road all loud and smoky. At any rate, the threat
to the business was definitely predictable.

So what went wrong? They failed to adapt.
As a newly minted cognoscenti of trust, you will
recognize this as a failure of competence.

The above example describes the method
for doing post-mortems on failed organizations. You take what is the purported reason
for their failure, and you dig a little deeper to
find the real cause of death. Surprisingly, the
elemental trust model works extremely well
for analyzing the pathology of trust.

Next, let's take a look at what the heck happened to organizations that fail in a big way.

## ORGANIZATIONAL TRUST FATALITIES

Within six months of the early twenty-first century, a tectonic trust shift occurred. Major institutions failed suddenly in three sectors—government, business, and nonprofit—with aftershocks still being felt ten years later. On September 11, 2001, the U.S. government failed to protect its citizens against terrorists. One month later, the Catholic Church sex abuse scandal was reported in the *Boston Globe.* Four months after that, the Enron scandal became public, breaching people's trust in financial executives, accounting firms, and government watchdog organizations. Stakeholders were left reeling as flood waters from these breaches spread globally and continued on for a decade.

These institutions failed us in a big way, with profound effects on a lot of people, yet institutional failure is surprisingly an understudied topic. Researchers typically look at failures of the individual organization, the market, business, or governance failures. A broad look

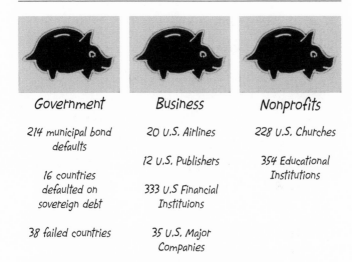

| Government | Business | Nonprofits |
|---|---|---|
| 214 municipal bond defaults | 20 U.S. Airlines | 228 U.S. Churches |
| 16 countries defaulted on sovereign debt | 12 U.S. Publishers | 354 Educational Institutions |
| 38 failed countries | 333 U.S Financial Instituions | |
| | 35 U.S. Major Companies | |

**FIGURE 16: Failed Institutions**

within and across government, business, and nonprofit sectors is rare.

I decided to do my own research study on institutional failure writ large. Just as we did in chapter 1, we start by defining our terms. Failure in the three sectors can be thought of as:

- Government failure: bond or sovereign debt default; or major failure from the failed state index[1]
- Business failure: bankruptcy or shutdown

---

1. Fund for Peace, 2012

- Nonprofit failure: major scandal or shutdown

For this research, I created a database of failed institutions. When I assessed them by sector, an interesting pattern with our elemental trust model showed up.

## FAILED INSTITUTIONS' CAUSE OF DEATH

The figure below lists the failed institutions in the database.

I was most suprised that so many governments had failed. After all, some of them collect their revenue with the power of the people with guns! We all know about Egypt and Libya, but so far in the first decade of the twenty-first century, thirty-eight countries have failed, either politically or economically with an additional sixteen defaulting on sovereign debt. In the U.S., 214 cities have defaulted on their municipal bonds—in just the past two years.

In the business sector, 333 financial institutions have failed in the first decade of this century. These include more than twenty U.S. airlines as well as companies like GM, Chrysler, Blockbuster, and Charter Communications. More than a dozen U.S. newspapers or magazine publishers have declared bankruptcy in the past three years alone.

Nonprofit sector institutional failures in my database include churches and schools. Despite this century's increase in people's self-reported

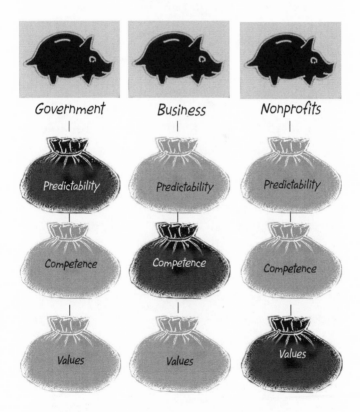

**FIGURE 16: Institutional Failure Alignment**

religiosity, 228 churches have folded and 350 Christian schools have shut down or merged with another institution, all within the last two years.[2] Four colleges closed down in the first ten years of this century, including Antioch College, founded in 1852, and McIntosh College, founded in 1896.

Next, I assessed the organizations in my failed institutions database using our elemental trust model. Each of the three trustworthiness factors—predictability, competence, and values—was assigned a color code: black for bad, white for good, grey for something in between. Some factors were left grey where no reliable information was available.

Next, I computed the average predictability, competence, and values ratings for the failed institutions within each sector: government, business, and nonprofit.

Now here's where it gets interesting. The black component for failed government sector institution was predictability; the black component for failed business sector institutions

---

2.   Parker, 2010

was competence; and the black component for failed nonprofit institutions was values. When I overlaid these ratings onto the earlier picture of failed institutions, the black factors line up perfectly with the sector, as shown below.

## GOVERNMENTS DIE ON PREDICTABILITY, BUSINESSES ON COMPETENCE, AND NONPROFITS ON VALUES

When I saw this result, I couldn't believe my eyes. How can a little old model that I came up with match the data so well? I suspected that I must be biased and set about looking for a way to *not* get such a clean validation of the trust model. I couldn't find anything.

On the face of it, doesn't it make sense that that incompetent businesses are more likely to fail than government or nonprofit institutions? The market is a superb indicator of competence—and a stern judge of incompetence. Perhaps nonprofit sector organizations, made up of more volunteers than other organizations, are more vulnerable to values that don't match expectations.

One implication of this pattern is that those interested in organizational failure might be able to focus their efforts more efficiently. Depending on the organization's sector, predictability, competence, or values might be a better predictor of failure than the other elements. As we say in the research business, more study is required in this area.

## PART II
# A Vision for the Future

*"Don't Underestimate the Power of a Vision."*
–K. Labich

TWELVE

# *Organizational Accountability*

## So What?

The early chapters of this book defined trust in a way that is easy and straightforward to understand. Using this definition, we've looked at trust breaches to find out just what the heck happened. In chapter 9, we described a three-step process to recover from breaches in interpersonal trust.

- STEP 1: Assess trust.
- STEP 2: Own your own piece of the problem.
- STEP 3: Do something.

Perhaps for you, the most useful thing to do with all this is to work on interpersonal trust breaches. You can think back on some situation where another person has really let you down, and rethink what the heck happened. Was it a failure of predictability? of competence? of values? Rather than concluding that you can't trust all [fill in the blank] you could pinpoint which of the trust factors was at the root of the problem. From there, you can focus your efforts to trust again without being stupid.

The interpersonal trust methodology describe above is relatively straightforward. The next two sections describe something a bit more complex: what you may be able to do to improve trust in organizations.

## IMPROVING
## ORGANIZATIONAL TRUSTWORTHINESS
### FROM *OUTSIDE* THE ORGANIZATION

You might be asking yourself, "what can I, a single person, do to affect trustworthiness of an organization? More than you think, and more than before. Let's apply our three-step process.

**STEP 1: Assessing Organizational Trust**

You probably don't need a lot of advice about this—you've experienced several untrustworthy organizations. Every time you are put on hold and a recorded voice tells you, "Your call is important to us," you've found an organization that is untrustworthy. Specifically, their integrity rates a "black" rating. If my call is so important to you, how about you get yourself more people to answer it?

We have gotten used to the slow erosion of organizational trustworthiness. Perhaps it doesn't hurt so much—doesn't feel like such a breach—when we realize that an organization slowly becomes less trustworthy.

Of course, you can spot an untrustworthy organization; you do it all the time. The other political party? They're always going back on their word. That bad meal? Incompetence. The kid selling candy bars with a suspicious looking man standing behind her? Questionable benevolence. You are clearly good at identifying untrustworthy organizations, but it takes time and experience.

Wouldn't it be nice if someone else could help you figure out who to trust? In some ways, this is happening already, in the form of failure. Those failed institutions we described earlier went under, in part, because they weren't trust-worthy. The voters/market/funders shut down those institutions.

Thank goodness, or we'd be living in a very icky world indeed.

Similarly, people are rating just about every-thing you can imagine via the internet. Origi-nally, online stores provided example of this, where sellers or buyers were given trust ratings to give an indication of their predictability.

So in addition to you being able to decide an organization's trustworthiness through our own experience, the internet provides a method for you to learn quickly from others' experience.

**STEP 2: Own Your Own Piece of the Problem.**

As described in Chapter 9, this is often the hardest part of the trust recovery process. When you have been ripped off, it is easy to see this as "all their fault." But there are things you could have done before the transaction, and things you can do afterwards. Beforehand, did you do your research? It takes a while to read customer reviews, and they may be off a bit, but on average, they are golden. Did you check all the details of the product/service/transaction? For instance, a seller's return policy, the shipping costs, etc.? The key is to break the trust breach down into lower-level elements. Then you can focus your ownership of your piece of the problem. This focusing lets you do two things: avoid repeating the problem the next time; and avoid concluding that a large category is untrustworthy. For instance, you could easily conclude that buying online is not to be repeated. If, instead, you realize that you neglected to check the shipping information (a lack of competence on your part), you might continue buying online, but more competently the next time.

## STEP 3: Do Something

After the transaction, it is very helpful for the rest of us if you go online and give a review. This is one of those areas where it doesn't benefit you as an individual, but you perform a community service to others if you take the time to write a review. Alternatively, there are the traditional ways of redressing your complaints—letters, calls, picketing stockholder meetings, and other fun activities. As mentioned above, breaking the trust breach down will help you. If you could have prevented the breach, then you know how to trust without being stupid the next time. If the breach was out of your control, then breaking down the breach will help you focus your efforts to avoid a similar breach.

## IMPROVING ORGANIZATIONAL TRUSTWORTHINESS FROM *WITHIN* THE ORGANIZATION

Why would you want to do this? Does it help the bottom line? There's evidence that it does, at least in online ratings. Recall that customers can go online and give ratings of 1-5 stars to sellers, depending on how satisfied they were. One study found that the last "star" in a seller's rating earned them 11 percent more sales price. That fifth star of trustworthiness is likely worth more than their less trustworthy competitor's entire profit margin.

Let's say you are a manager in, for instance,

a store. You've been there a while, since before the store went online. Before the online sales began, sales would decline but you wouldn't really know why. Sure, you had a few letters of complaint, and a few salespeople noticed some problems. What could you do? You could use your judgment to infer why sales were down. You were pretty good, but you didn't have much information.

Now, you have the online ratings, along with the written comments posted by those who bothered to write about their experience. The complaints are all over the place, and hard to sort through. Fortunately, our three-factor model helps you to categorize the information. You list the complaints and then assign them to either predictability, competence, or trust. One pops out as the source off almost all the complaints.

The value of this exercise is that you can focus your improvement efforts. You can spend money or manpower more efficiently if you have an idea of which of the three trust factors needs improvement.

You, the manager, can use customer feedback to pinpoint where you need to improve trustworthiness. Another way to use our three-factor model to improve is an internal evaluation. I have performed reengineering efforts where the root cause of cost and schedule problems is the fact that one part of the organization was acting in an untrustworthy way to another part. In one case, the testing guys didn't trust the manufacturing guys, because the manufacturing guys would deliver faulty hardware in order to claim on-time delivery. Later the manufacturing guys would take the hardware back to fix it. This messed up the testing guys' plans, but there was little they could do about it.

I have developed a trust assessment for use in internal evaluations. It is straightforward, easy to use, and gives a clear indication of what types of trust problems exist within an organization. It is amazing how significantly trust affects the bottom line, and how much happier employees are when they work in an environment of trust.

In this case, there was a predictability problem. The testing guys explained that if they knew when they would have good hardware that they could test, they would be able to plan.

Still another example comes from my board-room experience. I joined a board of trustees that was divided, philosophy-wise, into two groups. Every time there would be a vote, the results would be the same. We could accomplish very little because of our inability to discuss things rationally, and because of all the maneuvering by the majority party to stay in power. Because of our lack of trust in "the other" group, we were not doing our job.

## WE TRUSTEES COULDN'T TRUST.

Our CEO's contract was coming up and the board had a vital question to answer: did we trust the CEO? Originally, people said yes or no, they did or did not trust the CEO. It was hard to have a conversation, because everyone had a different definition of trust. Then we introduced the three-factor model. We found that there were some factors that were a problem for several members of the board. We ended up concluding that because of those "black" ratings, we did not trust the CEO. It was our first unanimous vote in years.

So not only did the three-factor model give

us a way of thinking about our trust, it helped us talk about our trust. From there, the model helped us make a decision to remove an untrustworthy leader.

# THIRTEEN

# Go for the Gold

It is difficult to put forth a vision, for they are fragile things, easily crushed by a careless misstep. I have a long history of setting forth visions—some say I am delusional but I nevertheless persist. Forgive me if I stretch imagination a bit past its comfort level, but bear with me for one final exposition.

I submit that it is hard for us to envision living in a trustworthy world—the so-called erosion of trust has been slow and insidious. But unless we start to envision what it might look like, we are not likely to get there. Let's look at little snapshots of what might be.

First, transactions are smoother. We spend an immense amount of money protecting ourselves against each other, and organizations spend even more protecting themselves from us. That twelve-page contract you sign when you buy a new car for cash used to be a handshake. The eight pages of 8-point font you are handed when you go to the hospital could be a bit less, don't you think?

Second, our individual energies could go into something productive, rather than something defensive. The cover-your-behind mentality slows things down. Similarly, organizations could be much more productive if they didn't have huge numbers of people protecting the organizations from, among other things, their employees. A large percentage of human resources, legal, and contracts professionals spend their time in protection mode, at the expense of productive mode.

Finally, people would be happier if there were more trust in the world. This assertion is hard to prove or quantify, but we all know it is true. We don't like thinking about being ripped off, do we? We'd much rather think about our families, our work, our hobbies.

While these three areas are general, the following lists some more tangible visions for what it might be like to live in a world of higher trust.

Imagine going into a business where they smile because they are delighted to see you again.

Imagine giving a little money to an organization that can right the wrongs you ran into, so that your kids, grandkids, and theirs-to-come won't have to learn that particular lesson the hard way.

Imagine being inspired by a leader so much that you want to quit your job and go work for that person.

I trust that you would enjoy living in such a world.

# Bibliography

Barker, R. (2011). Grizzly Shooting Becomes a Political Football. *Idaho Statesman* August 29, 2011.

Barney, J., & Hansen, M. (1994). Trustworthiness as a Source of Competitive Advantage. *Strategic Management Jounral*, 175-190.

Bhattacharya, R., Devinney, T. M., & Pillutla, M. M. (1998). A Formal Model of Trust Based on Outcomes. *The Academy of Management Review*, 459-472.

Bidner, C. & Francois, F. (2011). Cultivating Trust: Norms, Institutions, and the Implications of Scale. *The Economic Journal*, in press.

Bigley, G., & Pearce, J. (1998). Straining For Shared Meaning in Organization Science: Problems of Trust and Distrust. *the Academy of Management Review*, 405-421.

Bilsky, W., Janik, M., & Schwartz, S. (2010). The Structural Organization of Human Values: Evidence From Three Rounds of the European Social Survey (ESS). *Journal of Cross-Cultural Psychology* .

Bradach, J. L., & Eccles, R. G. (1989). Price, Authority, and Trust: From Ideal Types to Plural Forms. *Annual Review of Sociology*, 97-118.

Castaldo, S., Premazzi, K., & Zerbini, F. (2010). The Meaning (s) of Trust. A Content Analysis on the Diverse Conceptualizations of Trust in Scholarly Research on Business Relationships. *Journal of Business Ethics*, 657-668.

Cofta, P., & Hodgson, P. (2009). Designing for Trust for the Future Web. *Proceedings of the WebSci'09: Society On-Line.* Athens, Greece: In press.

Coleman, J. (1990). *Foundations of Social Theory.* Cambridge, MA: Belknap Press of Harvard University Press.

CNN (2002). Anderson Auditor Questioned Enron. April 2, 2002.

Crete, J., Pelletier, R., & Coutier, J. (2010). *Political Trust, Values, Performance and Media: A Canadian Profile.* National MPSA Conference, Chicago, IL.

Dasgupta, P. ( 1988 ). Trust As a Commodity. In D. G. Gambetta, *Trust* (pp. 49-72). New York: Basil Blackwell.

Deutsch. (1958). Trust and Suspicion. *Journal of Conflict Resolution*, 265-279.

Deutsch, M. (1958). Trust and Suspicion. *Journal of Conflict Resolution*, 265-279.

Ellison, C., & Firestone, I. (1974). Development of Interpersonal Trust as a Function of Self-Esteem, Target Status, and Target Style. *Journal of Personality and Social Psychology*, 655-663 .

Farris, G., Senner, E., & Butterfield, D. (1973). Trust, Culture, and Organizational Behavior. *Industrial Relations*, 144-157.

Frost, T., Stimpson, D. V., & Maughan, M. R. (1978). Some Correlates of Trust. *Journal of Psychology*, 103-108.

Fund for Peace (2012) Failed States Index. Website http://www.fundforpeace.org/global/?q=fsi accessed March 12, 2012.

Fukuyama, F. (1995). *Trust: The Social Virtues and the Creation of Prosperity.* New York: Simon & Schuster.

Gabarro, J. (1978 ). The Development of Trust, Influence, and Expectations. In A. Athos, & J. Gabarro, *Interpersonal Behavior: Communication and Understanding in Relationships* (pp. 290-303). Englewood Cliffs, NJ: Prentice Hall.

Gambetta, D. (1988). *Trust: Making and Breaking Cooperative Relations* . New York: NY: Blackwell.

Giffin, K. (1967). The Contribution of Studies of Source Credibility to a Theory of Interpersonal Trust in the Communication Department. *Psychological Bulletin*, 104-120.

Good, D. (1988). Individuals, Interpersonal Relations, and Trust. In D.G. Gambetta, *Trust* (pp. 131-185). New York: Basil Blackwell.

Gould, M. (2011). Idaho Man Faces Jail for Killing Grizzly Threatening Kids. *Newsmax* August 26, 2011.

Jenkins, G. J. *The Enron Collapse*. Upper Saddle River NJ: Prentice Hall, 2003.

Jones, G., & George, J. (1998). The Experience and Evolution of Trust: Implications for Cooperation and Teamwork. *The Academy of Management Review,*, 531-546.

Kee, H. W., & Knox, R. (1970). Conceptual and Methodological Considerations in the Study of Trust and Suspicion. *The Journal of Conflict Resolution*, 357-366.

Lee, H. (1960). *To Kill a Mockingbird*. New York: HarperCollins.

Lewicki, R., & Bunker, B. (1995). Trust in Relationships; A Model of Trust Development and Decline. In B. Bunker, & J. Rubin, *Conflict, Cooperation and Justice* (pp. 133-173). San Francisco: Jossey-Bass.

Lewis, J., & Weigert, A. ( 1985). Trust as a Social Reality. *Social Forces*, 967-985.

Limerick, D., & Cunnington, B. (1993). *Managing the New Organization*. San Francisco: Josee-Bass.

Luhmann, N. (1979). *Trust and Power*. New York: Wiley.

Manor, R. and J. Yates (2002). Faceless Anderson Partner in Spotlight's Glare. *The Chicago Tribune* April 14, 2002.

Mayer, R. C., Davis, J. H., & Schoorman, F. D. (1995). An Integrative Model of Organizational Trust. *Academy of Management Review*, 709-734.

McKnight, D. H., & Chervany, N. L. (2001). *The Meaning of Trust (Working Paper)*. Retrieved March 9, 2011, from http://www.misrc.umn.edu/wpaper/wp96-04.htm

McKnight, D., & Chervany, N. (2008). Reflections on an Initial Trust-Building Model. In A. Zaheer, *Handbook of Trust Research* (pp. 29-51).

Merriam-Webster. (n.d.). *Merriam-Webster Dictionary.* Retrieved March 16, 2011, from M-W.com: http://www.merriam-webster.com/dictionary/trust

Mishra, A. K. (1996). Organizational Responses to Crisis: The Centrality of Trust . In R. Kramer, & T. Tyler, *Trust in organizations* (pp. 261-287 ). Thousand Oaks, CA: Sage.

Oxford Advanced Learner's Dictionary. (n.d.). *open-minded.* Retrieved 3 20, 2011, from *Oxford Advanced Learners' Dictionary*: http://www.oxfordadvancedlearnersdictionary.com/dictionary/open-minded

Oxford-English Dictionary. (n.d.). *Oxford-English Dictionary.* Retrieved March 16, 2011, from http://wiki.uni.lu/secan-lab/Trust+%28$28%29Oxford+English+Dictionary%28$29%29.html

PBS (2002) Interview: Joseph Berardino, May 1, 2002.

Rogala, J., & Orsborn, C. (2005). Trust, Inc.: A Practical Guide to the Alignment of Values, Organizational Goals and Results. Chicago, IL: Ampersand, Inc.

Rotter, J. B. (1967). A New Scale for the Measurement of Interpersonal Trust. *Journal of Personality*, 651-665.

Rotter, J. (1971). Generalized Expectancies for Interpersonal Trust. *American Psychologist*, 443-452.

Rotter, J. (1980). Interpersonal Trust, Trustworthiness and Gullibility. *American Psychologist*, 1-7.

Rousseah, D., Sitkin, S., Burt, R., & Camerer, C. (1998). Not so Different After All: A Cross-Discipline View of Trust. *Academy of Management Review*, 393-404.

Schoorman, F. D., Mayer, R., & Davis, J. (2007). An Integrative Model of Organizational Trust: Past, Present, and Future. *Academy of Management Review*, 344–354.

Schwartz, S. (1992). Universals in the Content and Structure of Values: Theoretical Advances and Empirical Tests in 20 Countries. *Advances in Experimental Social Psychology*, 1-65.

Schwartz, S., & Boehnke, K. (2004). Evaluating the Structure of Human Values. *Journal of Research in Personality*, 230-255.

Sen, S., & Chakraborty, K. (2010). Comprehensive Trust Management. *Proceedings of the 9th International Conference on Autonomous Agents and Multiagent Systems* (pp. 1573-1574). Toronto, Canada: International Foundation for Autonomous Agents and Multiagent Systems.

Shockley-Zalabak, P., Morreale, S., & Hackman, M. (2010). *Building the High-Trust Organization: Strategies for Supporting Five Key Dimensions of Trust*. San Francisco, CA: Wiley.

Tschannen-Moran, M., & Hoy, W. (2000). A Multidisciplinary Analysis of the Nature, Meaning, and Measurement of Trust. *Review of Educational Research*, 547-593.

Tyler, T., & Kramer, R. (1996). Whither trust? In R. Kramer, & T. (. Tyler, *Trust in Organizations* (pp. 1-15). Thousand Oaks, CA: Sage.

Viljanen, L. (2005). Towards an Ontology of Trust. In S. Katsikas, L. J., & P. G. (Eds.), *Trust, Privacy, and Security in Digital Business* (pp. 175-184). Springer-Verlag.

Wainfan, L. (2010). *Multi-perspective Strategic Decision Making: Principles, Methods, and Tools*. Santa Monica, CA: Doctoral Dissertation: the RAND Corporation.

Zuckerman, L. (2011). Prosecution for Fatal Grizzly Prosecution Sparks Debate. *Reuters* August 29, 2011.

Made in the USA
San Bernardino, CA
09 December 2013